SCHOLASTIC

News

Nonfiction Readers

Beavers

And Other Animals With Amazing Teeth

by
Susan Labella

Children's Press®
A Division of Scholastic Inc.
New York Toronto London Auckland Sydney
Mexico City New Delhi Hong Kong
Danbury, Connecticut

These content vocabulary word builders
are for grades 1-2.

Consultant: Sharon T. Brown, M.A.
Wildlife Biologist
Beavers: Wetlands & Wildlife

Reading Specialist: Don Curry

Special thanks to Omaha's Henry Doorly Zoo

Photo Credits:

Photographs 2005: Corbis Images: 23 bottom right (Steve Kaufman), cover background (Paul A. Souders), 15 (Kennan Ward); Dembinsky Photo Assoc.: back cover, 4 top right (Mary Clay), cover right inset, 5 bottom left, 19 (Marilyn & Maris Kazmers), 2, 4 bottom right, 10, 21 bottom (Bruce Montague); Getty Images: 20 right, 21 left (Geostock/PhotoDisc Green), 23 top left (John Lund/The Image Bank); Minden Pictures: 23 top right (Michael & Patricia Fogden), cover center inset, 16 (Frans Lanting); NHPA: 5 top left, 17 (Martin Harvey), 20 center left (Rich Kirchner); Photo Researchers, NY: 23 bottom left (Sylvain Cordier), 20 bottom (Harry Engels), 4 left, 8, 22 (Leonard Lee Rue III), 21 top right (Tom & Pat Leeson), 5 top right, 14 (Tom McHugh); Photolibrary.com/Norbert Rosing: 20 top left; Seapics.com: 18 (Doug Perrine), 13 (Kevin Schafer), cover left inset, 5 bottom right, 12 (Doc White); Visuals Unlimited: 1, 9 (Carlyn Galati), 7 (Science VU).

Book Design: Simonsays Design!

Library of Congress Cataloging-in-Publication Data

Labella, Susan, 1948-
    Beavers and other animals with amazing teeth / by Susan LaBella.
        p. cm. – (Scholastic news nonfiction readers)
    Includes bibliographical references (p.   ) and index.
    ISBN 0-516-24930-4 (lib. bdg.)   0-516-24776-X (pbk.)
    1. Teeth–Juvenile literature. I. Title. II. Series.
    QL858.L33 2005
    599.37–dc22

                                                    2005002097

1 2 3 4 5 6 7 8 9 10 R 14 13 12 11 10 09 08 07 06 05

CONTENTS

Word Hunt 4-5

Teeth! Teeth! 6-7

Beaver Teeth 8-9

More About Beaver Teeth 10-11

Walrus Teeth 12-13

Snake Teeth 14-15

Crocodile Teeth 16-17

Shark Teeth 18-19

Busy Beaver Teeth! 20-21

Your New Words 22

**These Animals Have
   Amazing Teeth, Too!** 23

Index 24

Find out More 24

Meet the Author 24

WORD HUNT

Look for these words as you read. They will be in **bold**.

beaver
(**bee**-ver)

incisors
(in-**sye**-zuhrs)

lodge
(loj)

crocodile
(**krok**-uh-dile)

fangs
(fangs)

shark
(shark)

tusks
(tusks)

Teeth! Teeth!

How do animals use their teeth?

Some animals use their teeth to chew or bite.

Some use their teeth to build homes.

Let's look at some animals that have amazing teeth!

This beaver has almost cut down this tree!

7

A **beaver** has four front teeth. These teeth are called **incisors**.

The beaver uses its incisors to gnaw on trees.

When it gnaws, its incisors get shorter. So, its teeth have to keep growing.

incisors

This beaver uses its teeth
to cut down a tree.

This beaver is using its teeth to eat. It's eating the green bark on a tree branch.

The beaver can use the branches to build a **lodge**.

The beaver lives in the lodge.

lodge

A walrus has teeth, too. It has two **tusks**.

Tusks are long teeth that stick out of its mouth.

It uses its tusks to pull itself out of the water onto the ice.

tusks

Some snakes have teeth called **fangs**.

Some snakes are poisonous.

After a snake bites an animal, the poison runs through the fangs into the animal.

The poison hurts the animal.

fangs

This is a rattlesnake.
It is poisonous.

A **crocodile** has teeth shaped like cones.

First, a crocodile catches an animal with its teeth.

Then, it eats the animal whole.

tooth

This crocodile catches a fish to eat.

A shark has many rows of sharp teeth.

Sharp teeth help a **shark** catch food.

If a shark's tooth falls out, another tooth moves into its place.

tooth

This shark has lots of teeth.

BUSY BEAVER TEETH!
How Does A Beaver Build Its Home?

1...

First, the beaver makes a dam. It uses its sharp teeth to drag logs into the water.

2...

The dam is made of sticks and mud. The dam will protect the beaver's home.

3...

Next, the beaver builds its lodge. It uses its teeth to cut the logs.

5

Now, it's time to eat! The beaver and its babies are inside the lodge. The beaver grinds a tree branch with its teeth.

4 The lodge looks like this.

21

YOUR NEW WORDS

beaver (**bee**-ver) an animal with a wide, flat tail that lives on land and in water

crocodile (**krok**-oh-dile) a large reptile with short legs and strong jaws

fangs (fangs) fangs are long, pointed teeth

incisors (in-**sye**-zuhrs) a beaver has four front teeth called incisors

lodge (loj) a lodge is a beaver's home

shark (shark) a large fish with very sharp teeth that eats meat

tusks (tusks) the teeth of a walrus are called tusks